HYMNS FOR WO

17 Intermediate piano solos
Church Preludes, Offertories, and Communion

Arranged by Julie A. Lind

CONTENTS

Julie Lind gives churches permission to perform her arrangements in church services, including live and recorded services on all online platforms.

Let All Things Now Living

Welsh Folk Tune
Arranged by Julie A. Lind

21
2
4
1
f
26
31
mf
1
2
1
35
39
mp
rit.

Great Is Thy Faithfulness

Music by William M. Runyan
Arranged by Julie A. Lind

17
mf

21

25

29

33

37
f

41
mp

45

This Is My Father's World

Traditional English Melody
Adapted by Franklin Sheppard
Arranged by Julie A. Lind

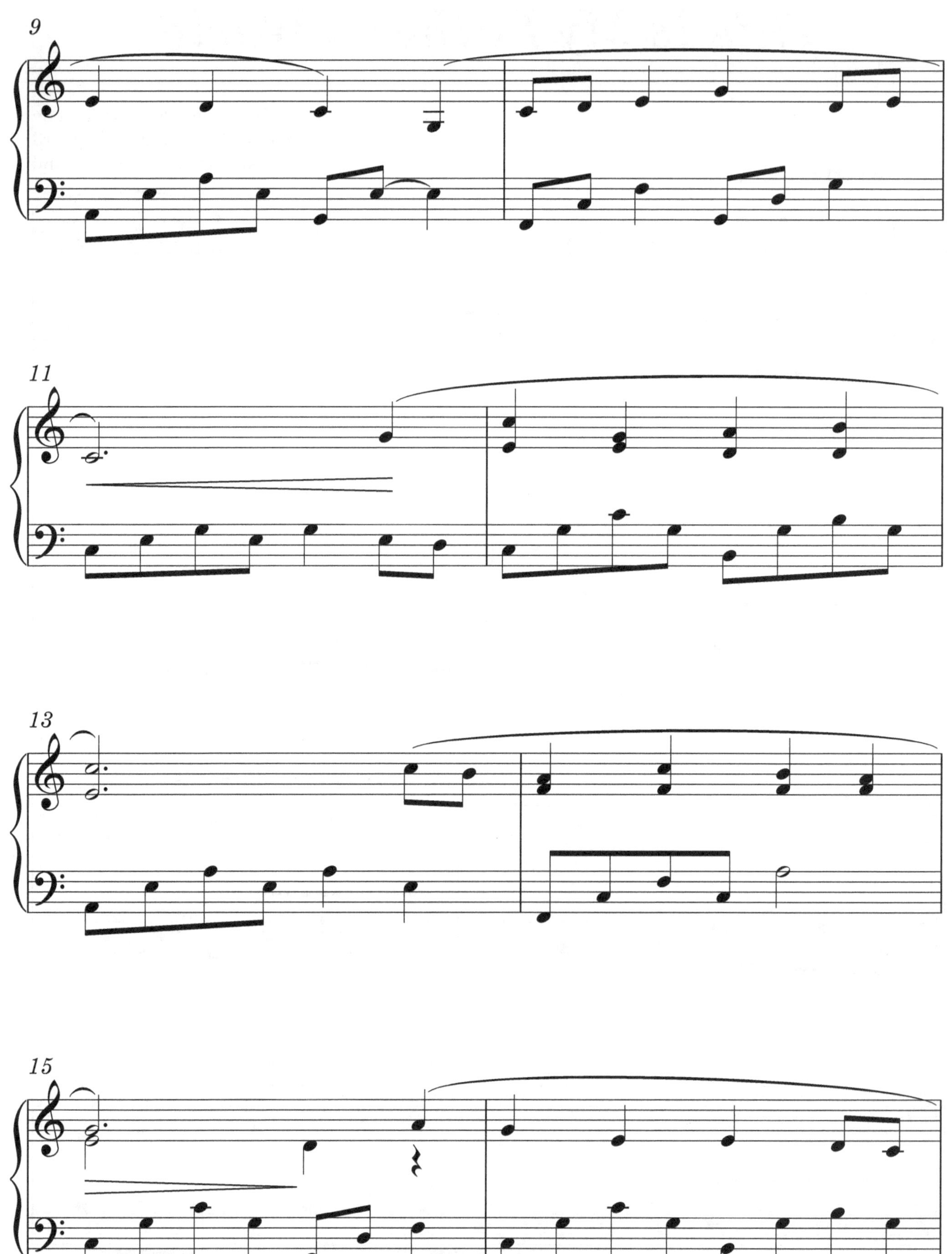
9
11
13
15

17

19
mp

21
1.
mf

23
2.
rit.
p

Jesus Loves Me

Traditional
Arranged by Julie A. Lind

12
15
18
mp
20
rit.
p

Lord, I Want to be a Christian

Traditional Spiritual
Arranged by Julie A. Lind

13

16
mf

19

22

25

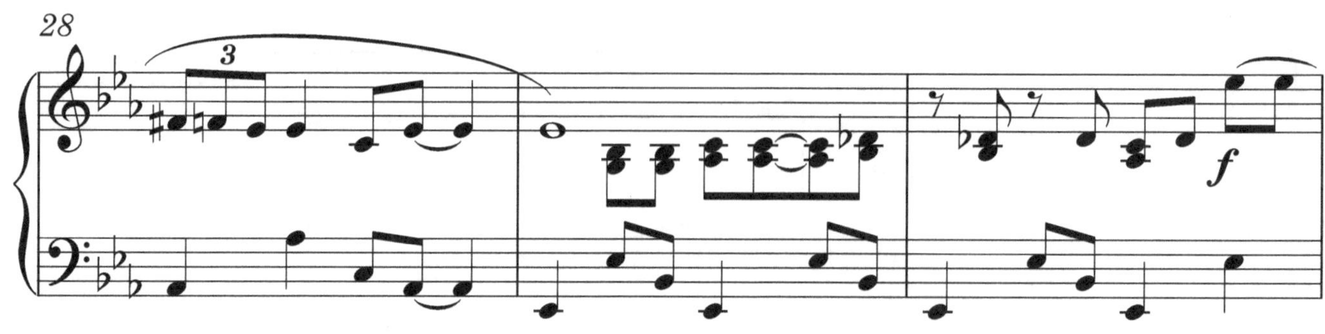
28
3
f

31

34
3

37
mf

40
f

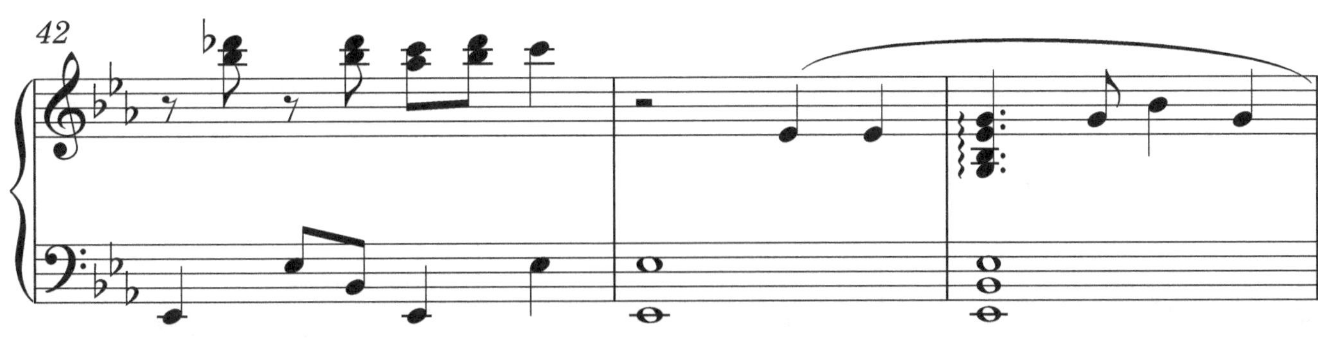
42

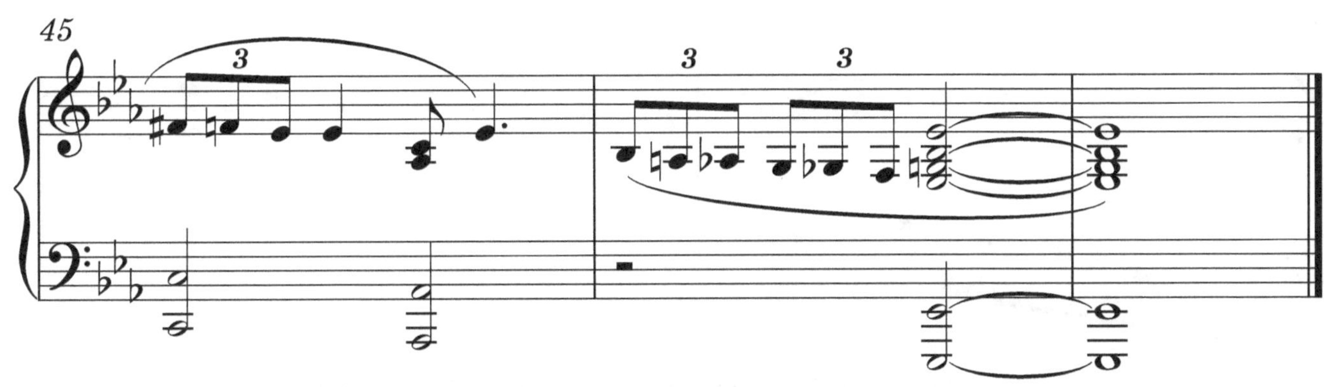
45
3
3
3

Fairest Lord Jesus

Traditional Hymn
Arranged by Julie A. Lind

12
3
1

15

18

21

For the Beauty of the Earth

Conrad Kocher
Arranged by Julie A. Lind

9
11
13
2
15
3
17

19

21

23

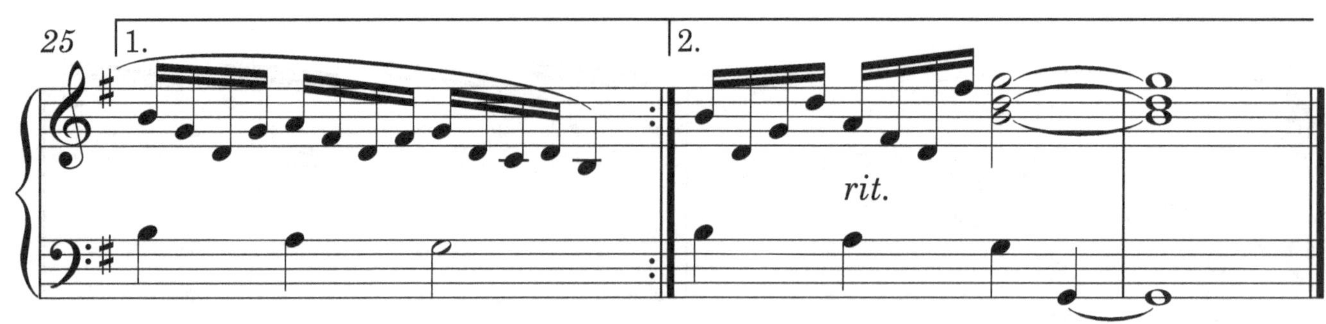
25
1.
2.
rit.

He Leadeth Me

William Bradbury
Arranged by Julie A. Lind

11
f

14

17

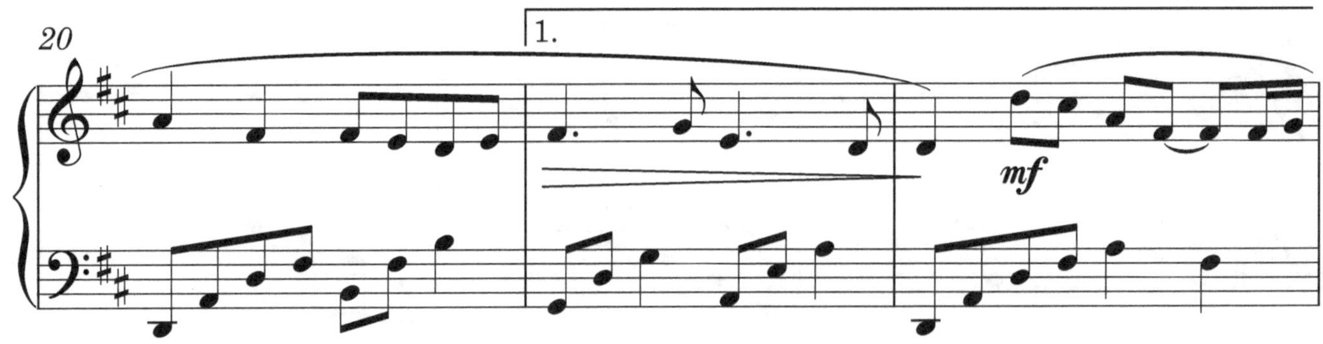
20
1.
mf

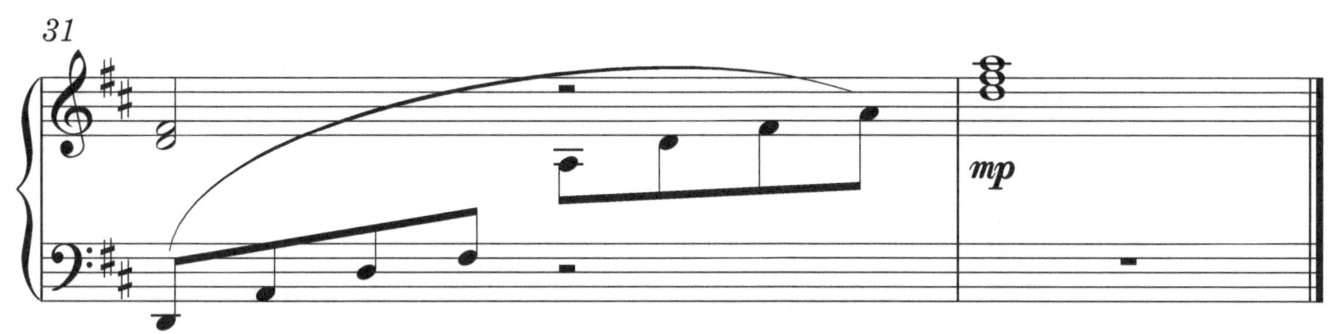
23
26
2.
29
rit.
31
mp

What a Friend We Have in Jesus

Charles Convers
Arranged by Julie A. Lind

13
16
19
f
22
25
mf

28
31
34
f
37
mf
39
mp

Abide with Me

Music by William H. Monk (Eventide)
Arranged by Julie A. Lind

9
mf

12

15

18

21
24
27
30
mp

Go, My Children, with My Blessing

Welsh Traditional
Arranged by Julie A. Lind

9
f

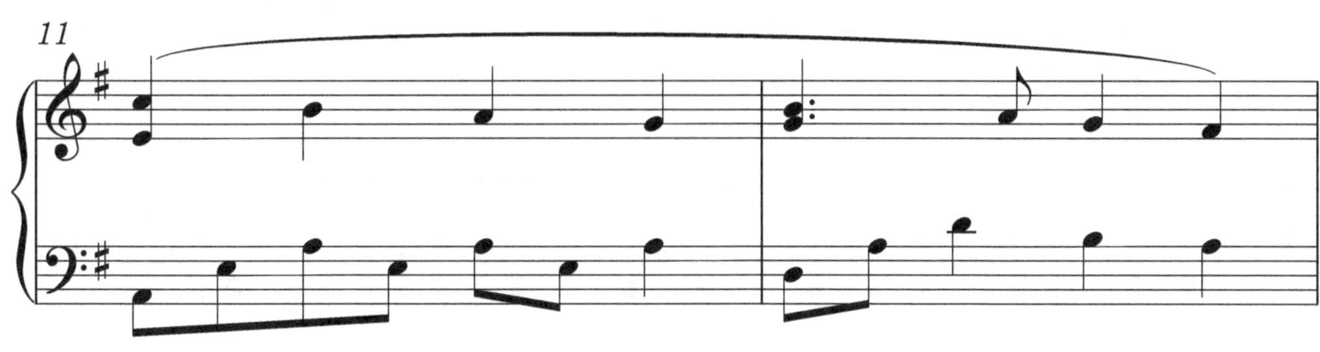
11

13
mf

15

Just As I Am

William B. Bradbury
Arranged by Julie A. Lind

16

20

24
1.

27
2.
rit.

Give Me Jesus

African American Spiritual
Arranged by Julie A. Lind

9
f
11
mf
13
15
1.
2.

When I Survey the Wondrous Cross

Isaac Watts
Arranged by Julie A. Lind

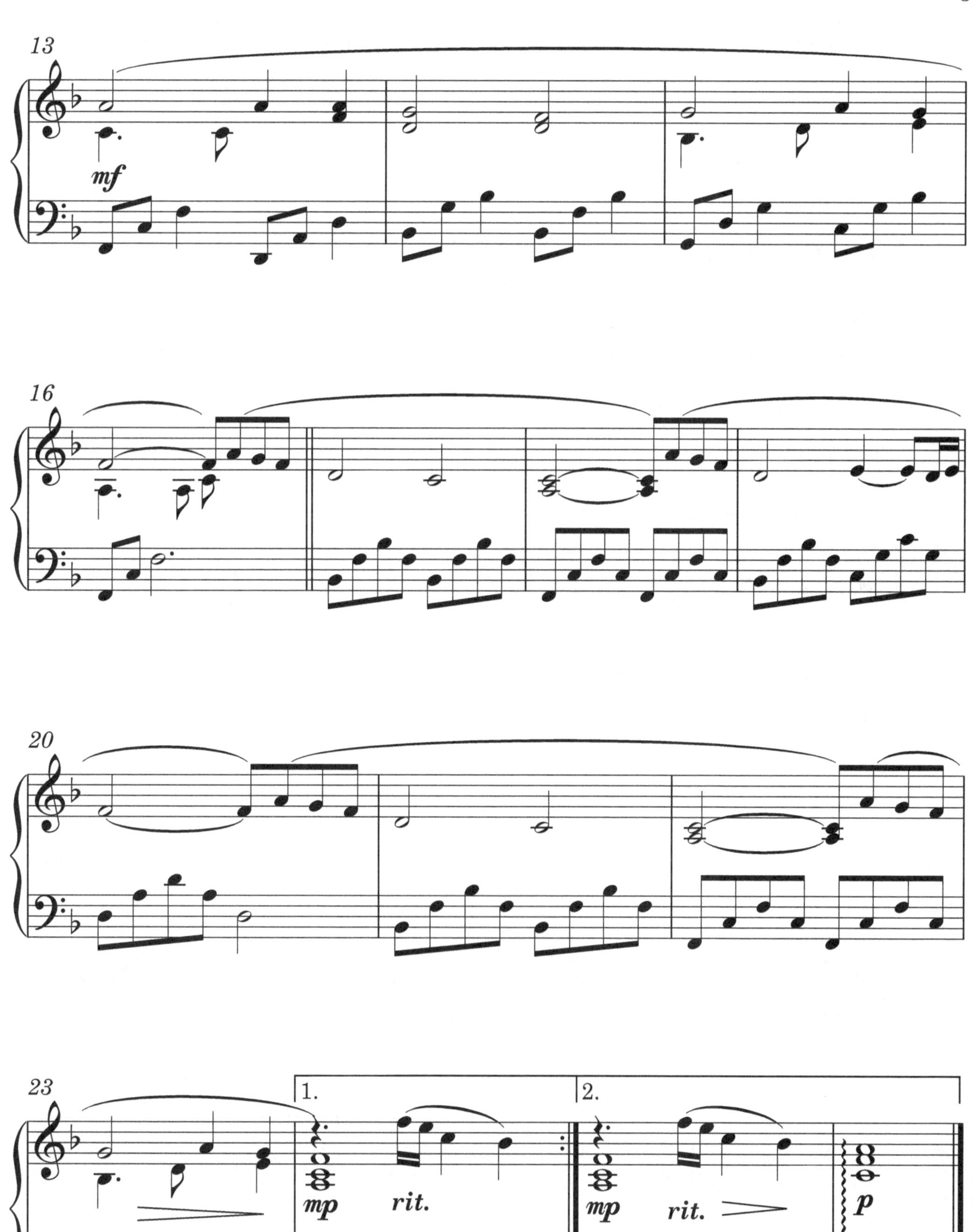
13
mf
16
20
23
1.
mp
rit.
2.
mp
rit.
p

What Wondrous Love is This

Tune by W. Walker
Arranged by Julie A. Lind

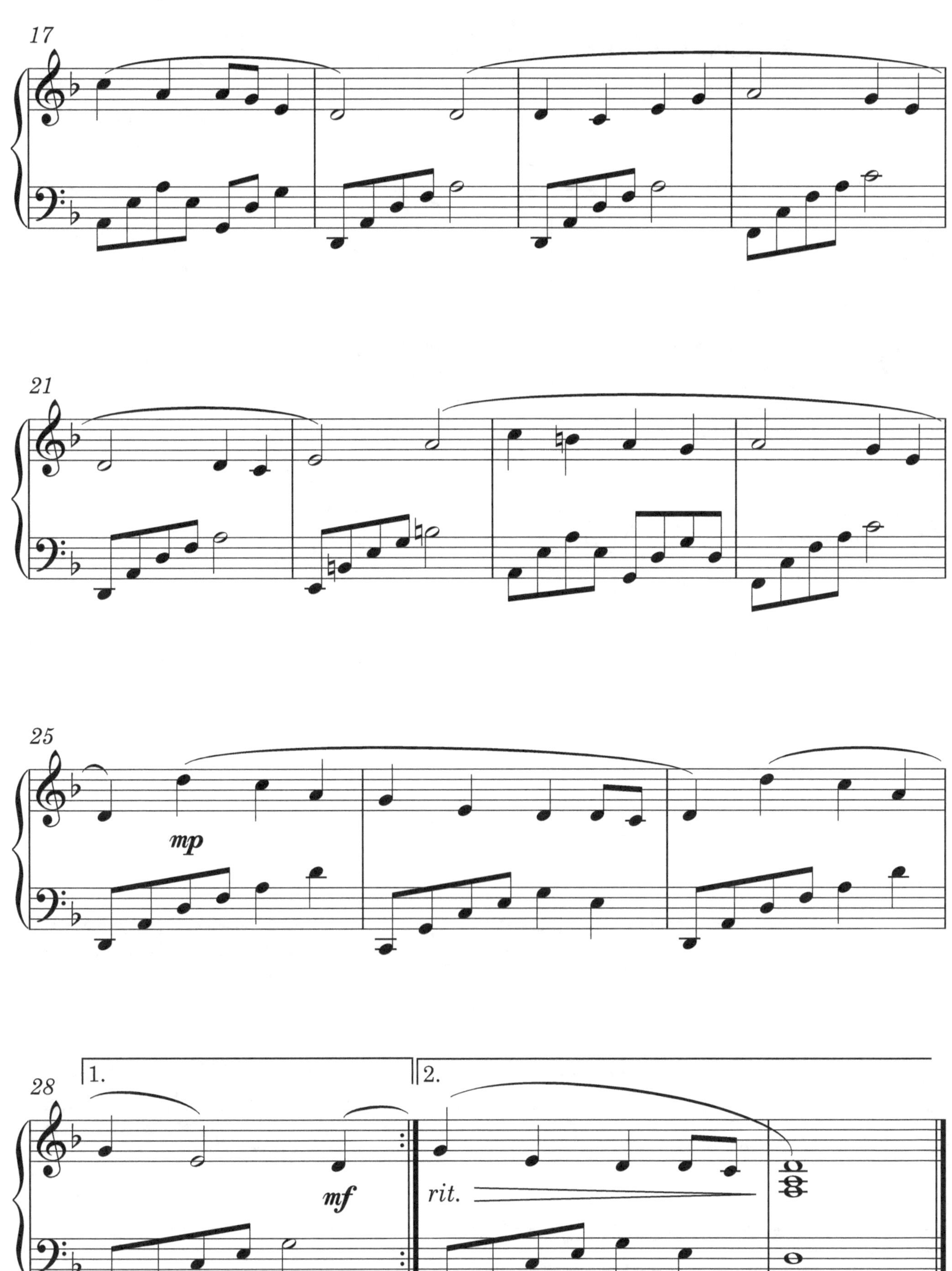
17
21
25
mp
28
1.
2.
mf
rit.

I Love to Tell the Story

William G. Fischer
Arranged by Julie A. Lind

13
3
3
16
19
22

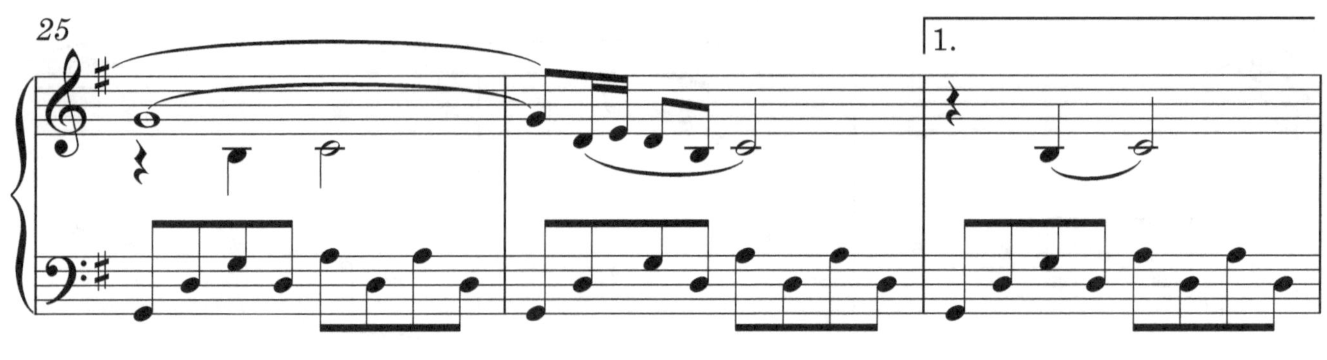
25
1.

28
2.

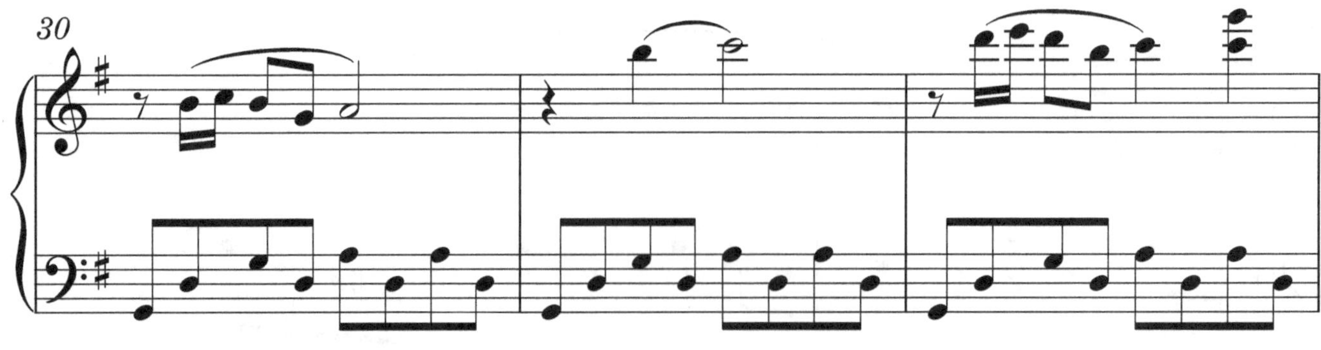
30

33
8va
mp
8va

Were You There?

Traditional Spiritual
Arranged by Julie A. Lind

9
12
15
17
p
mf
p

19
mf
mp
22
24
1.
27
2.
rit.
p

Made in United States
Troutdale, OR
02/20/2024

17828963R00027